Change Management

90 Minute Guides

Michelle N. Halsey

Copyright © 2016 Silver City Publications & Training, L.L.C.

Silver City Publications & Training, L.L.C.
P.O. Box 1914
Nampa, ID 83653
https://www.silvercitypublications.com/shop/

ISBN-10: 1-64004-010-2
ISBN-13: 978-1-64004-010-6

Contents

Chapter 1 - Change Management

Change is a constant in many of our lives. All around us, technologies, processes, people, ideas, and methods often change, affecting the way we perform daily tasks and live our lives. This workshop will give any leader tools to implement changes more smoothly and to have those changes better accepted. This workshop will also give all participants an understanding of how change is implemented and some tools for managing their reactions to change.

By the end of this chapter, you should be able to:

- List the steps necessary for preparing a change strategy and building support for the change

- Describe the WIFM – the individual motivators for change

- Use needed components to develop a change management and communications plans, and to list implementation strategies

- Employ strategies for gathering data, addressing concerns and issues, evaluating options and adapting a change direction

- Utilize methods for leading change project status meetings, celebrating a successful change implementation, and sharing the results and benefits

- Describe the four states of Appreciative Inquiry, its purposes, and sample uses in case studies

- Use strategies for aligning people with a change, appealing to emotions and facts

- Describe the importance of resiliency in the context of change, and employ strategies the change leader and individual change participant can use to foster resiliency

- Explain the importance of flexibility in the context of change, and demonstrate methods the change leader and individual change participant can use to promote flexibility

Preparing for Change

A simple definition of change is "to cause to be different". The idea of change management on a personal level has been studied for more than one hundred years. But it is only since the mid- 1980's that change management has been explored within the context of business applications.

Today's change management initiatives have become a business discipline, driving bottom-line results through changes in systems and behaviors. Managing change has therefore become a critical skill, both for leadership -- and for workers in an organization.

Defining Your Strategy

It is critical to manage change by creating and implementing a strategy that defines an approach consistent with the unique needs of the organization. The strategy serves as the guiding framework, providing direction and shaping decision making throughout the change process.

A simple way to gather data for the strategy is to set up interviews and ask questions regarding the different aspects of the change. Below are some typical questions:

Aspect	Question
The Situation	What is being changed? How much perceived need for the change exists? What groups will be impacted? How long will the change take?
People and their Roles	Who will serve as a high-level sponsor? What functional groups should be represented to lead the effort?
Issues for Analysis	What will happen if we do/don't do this? How universal is the change? Are there exceptions or deviations to consider?

From the answers to the questions, the strategy document is created, serving as a "blueprint" for the initiative. A strategy document should discuss important components of the change. The components are listed below, accompanied by sample wording.

Strategy Component	Sample Language / Notes
Description of the proposed change vision, and its goals	Transform the business processes and the technology by which the organization manages the human resources and payroll functions
The reasons(s) why the change is necessary	These changes will allow the organization to save time and money and provide more responsive HR and payroll services to our employees
Critical success measures and key performance indicators	Risks have been proactively identified and addressed Employees are prepared to perform their new job on Go live day with a 95% success ratio
Project stakeholders and stakeholder groups and their involvement	The current Phase: Senior management The Pre-Implementation Phase: Senior management, subject matter experts, change champions
Key messages to communicate	Pre-Implementation Phase: The business requirements, business case staffing, and the projected timeline
Roles and Responsibilities	Communications Team Lead: Develop project communications and presentations Change Management Team Lead: Direct overall team activities; Provide team with change management expertise; Manage Project Team Effectiveness, Capability Transfer, & Leadership Alignment activities
Target time frame to achieve goals	(This can be a graphical time line, a paragraph, an embedded spreadsheet, etc.)
Focus Areas	Leadership Alignment: Align leaders to the project vision and enable them to champion the effort Organizational transition: Design new employee roles, jobs, and organization structures to support the new processes and technology

Building the Team

To effectively implement a team positioned for success, leaders must select members who display a high degree of skill in six key elements:

- Commitment

- Contribution

- Communication

- Cooperation

- Conflict management

- Connection

The team must represent all of the needed functional groups and roles necessary to manage the change initiative. By formalizing the team and providing funding and other resources, it sends a message of accountability and responsibility, and illustrates the investment the organization has made in the change.

Chapter 2 – Identifying the WIFM

For change to be successful, people must desire to support and participate in the change. Simply building awareness does not generate desire. Showing everyone what is in it for them will produce a great starting point and help generate support. The beginning of the change process is very important and showing the affected parties how the change will improve their environment will initiate the process on the right foot.

What's in it for Me?

In order to answer the question "What's in it for Me?", or WIFM, change management leadership must create energy and engagement around the change. This builds momentum, and instills support at all levels of the organization. Factors that influence WIFM are:

- The nature of the change

- The organizational context for the change

- An employee's personal situation

- What motivates the person as an individual?

The next exercise provides data input that can be used to discover what's in the change for employees at Contemporary Chemical.

Building Support

Effective communications are essential for building support throughout the organization.

Whoever communicates with people impacted by a change must have a clear understanding of the overall nature of the change, its reasons, and how it aligns with the vision for the organization. He or she must understand the risks of not changing, the timing for the change, and what people will be most impacted by the change.

Communications options are many, including email, presentations, postings on the organization's intranet, flyers and circulars, banners, online or phone conferences, and special social events.

Beforehand, communicators should identify and segment audience groups, craft messages appropriate for each audience, and determine the most effective packaging, timing, and methods for communicating.

- Executive sponsorship

- Coaching by managers and supervisors

- Ready access to business information

Chapter 3 – Understanding Change

Change is constant and will always occur, and understanding its components on an individual level can help us relate it to an organizational level. Change is important to understand, as it affects many facets of an organization. Its effect on the individual is of great importance as it will filter through and influence all levels of the organization. Organizational change can create fear and uncertainty, it is important to understand these influences; what is expected when they do occur, and preparing for them when they happen.

Influences on Change

Typically causes of change can be split into two categories: Internal and External.

No organization is an island and external forces are always influencing and interacting with its existence. Individuals and organizations may have very little ability to influence such external factors such as politics, culture, economy, societal changes, or technology. It is important to understand that if the change is the result of an external factor, accept the change, and then modify any internal processes or items that are affected by the external influence.

Internal factors are very numerous, as almost any item or event can influence change within an organization, but some of the more influential ones are employees, policies, organization structure, managerial, and financial. With internal causes of change we have the most ability to control and prepare the outcomes of such events. The benefits of this are numerous as we can prepare with education, communication, training, and support. These tools will help mitigate any negative outcomes which may occur as a result of the change.

Common Reactions to Change

- **Denial:** If a change is announced some people may feel that the change is not necessary. They may be reluctant to listen or deny any facts or information presented to support the change.

- **Resistance**: With any change there will always be people who resist the change. Resistance is very common and stems from a fear of the unknown. Not knowing how an event is going to turn out can be a scary event for those who go through the change.

- **Anger:** When change occurs and the norm is uprooted, people can experience anger. People may lash out and become uncooperative during this time. Humans are creatures of habit, and when that changes people can become angry.

- **Indifference:** People just may not care, or the change may not have an impact on their routines or work. Be wary of this, as the change may be intended to have an impact, if the individual is indifferent about it the change then they may not understand or accept it.

- **Acceptance:** Changes generally occur for the better and have a positive influence on those involved. Even with positive change acceptance may not happen right away, but should occur quicker as opposed to when the change is perceived to be negative.

Tools to Help the Change Process

Preparing for the change is very important as with preparation comes more chance of success. These tools will help facilitate the change process and provide it the best chances for success.

- **Communication**: Keep the lines of communication open before, during and after the change as on the fly changes may be needed. This will help with any unforeseen events that occur during the change. It will also help to learn for the event which should make future changes occur even smoother.

- **Education**: Educate all parties the reasons for the change, and what the expected outcomes will be. People want to know why a change is occurring. It will also help to stop and clear up any rumors that may have been spread.

- **Training:** Make sure all parties are trained and up to date with any and all material required for the change. A very important step if the change involves adding or removing any pertinent in the business.

- **Flexibility**: When change is planned for not all events can be foreseen. Be flexible and ready to modify or update the current plan to account for any unforeseen events.

- **Affected Parties**: It is especially important to have the individuals that are involved in the change participate in the change process. They may be able to shed light into the subject from an expert's point of view.

These tools will help battle any negative reactions when they occur, and with more preparation the change should be smoother.

Chapter 4 – Leading and Managing the Change

Every change begins with a leadership decision. Making the decision to institute changes is not always easy. Being prepared, planning well, and being surrounded by a good team will make that decision a lot easier.

Preparing and Planning

Begin by putting yourself in a positive frame of mind. You are likely to experience higher than normal levels of stress and knowing this beforehand will give you the ability to be prepared mentally and physically. You will be the anchorperson and foundation, and with your steady hand will guide your team through the stressful events. Be a reassuring and active force throughout the whole process.

It is impossible to prepare for every contingency, but planning for the known is a must. Add time or extra room to the schedule for the unknowns. When you encounter an unexpected event your schedule should not be put off by much if you have built in some leeway. It will provide that buffer that gives you and your team the ability to deal with the unknowns and keep rolling with the change process.

Delegating

Surround yourself with people that you can delegate to and be confident in their abilities and skills. Be precise and specific with your directions as when the change process begins you will be depending on these individuals and their talents. Communicating and providing feedback are the keys to successful delegation; make sure your team understands this. If communication fails or there is not accurate feedback the chances of a success are lessened.

An issue that sometimes arises when delegating is micro-managing. Keep an eye out to not micro-manage as you can quickly lose track of events and it will take time away from your main duties. Delegating is a skill that takes time as you must first learn the strengths and weakness of your team and know what tasks you can and cannot hand out. It may not be possible to always delegate, but when it can be done it will provide a great resource.

Keep the Lines of Communication Open

Always be available during the change process. Before the change prepare your friends and family that you may not be available for social events. Reassure your team that you are there for them and you are here to provide them with the necessary resources to lead them through the change. Stress to them that you are available and focused on keeping the communications lines open.

Always be aware of rumors, they will happen before during and after the change. Do not ignore any rumor, put out honest and clear communication as soon as possible. Reassure your team that if they hear a rumor to seek out more information from a reliable source. Remind them that spreading rumors helps no one and will causes more harm than good.

Coping with Pushback

Not everyone will agree on the change. Keep in mind that these types of feelings are normal as people generally do not enjoy change and are sometimes made nervous by it. You will likely encounter pushback and resistance by a number of team members. Provide facts and data to show why the change is happening and reassure them the need and benefits of the change. These types of individuals are best suited to be educated about the change with information.

If you are encountering an extreme case of pushback, provide them with some choices that still fall within the spectrum of the intended change. They should then feel more involved in the process and it will help alleviate the negative mindset they may be experiencing.

Chapter 5 – Gaining Support

It is vitally important to make sure that all stakeholders and employees are on board with a change.

Gathering Data

In order to continue increasing awareness and to build desire to support the upcoming change; the change management team must reach out to the organization at large. The force field analysis, developed by German social psychologist Kurt Lewin helps a change management team to:

- Identify pros and cons of an option prior to making a decision

- Explore what is going right -- and what is going wrong

- Analyze any two opposing positions.

Addressing Concerns and Issues

If concerns or issues arise, then steps must be taken to ensure awareness is continually raised and that desire to support the change is increased. Strategies that can help the change management team responsively address employees' concerns include:

- Engaging employees, providing forums for people to express their questions and concerns

- Equipping managers & supervisors to be effective change leaders and managers of resistance

- Orchestrating opportunities for advocates of the change to contact those not yet on board

- Aligning incentive and performance management systems to support the change.

Evaluating and Adapting

Change is not exempt from Murphy's Law. And even if something isn't going wrong, change management team members must constantly be observing, listening, and evaluating the progress and process during a change. Below are several tools to help the team accomplish this.

A feedback form is used to gather information from those involved in a change to help shape the remaining course of the change project. Instead of a paper form, feedback can be obtained through online surveys (Zoomerang.com or Survey Monkey.com), an in-house questionnaire on the intranet, a few questions sent by email, or a focus group. The questions will vary depending upon the subject being queried.

Open Feedback:

Please feel free to share your suggestions and comments

The compiled results of the feedback forms can be used by the change management team members to modify the project plan and/or the communication plan or to work with specific individuals or groups that may be providing roadblocks to success.

Chapter 6 – Making It All Worthwhile

Once a change initiative is underway, it is critical to sustain the change with reinforcement.

Leading Status Meetings

The leader must make sure that the project and communication plan remain on track. They need to identify, and explore any issues from employees or stakeholders that have emerged, and review and consider any feedback gathered to date.

Acting as a facilitator, the leader helps to bring about learning and productivity. Communication will be a byproduct of this by providing indirect or unobtrusive assistance, guidance, and supervision.

He or she listens actively, asks questions, encourages diverse viewpoints, organizes information, helps the group reach consensus, and understands that the individual needs of team members will affect teamwork.

The LEAD model provides a simple methodology for facilitating a participative meeting:

- **Lead with objectives**: When clear objectives are stated up front, group energy is channeled toward achieving an outcome. The objectives shape the content of the meeting.

- **Empower to participate:** In the Lead model, the facilitator is empowered to encourage active participation.

- **Aim for consensus:** Getting the team to consensus will have members more likely to support and carry out the decisions of the team.

- **Direct the process:** How the meeting progresses will influence the quality of the decisions of the team, and influences the commitment of team members.

Leaders must differentiate between process and content. *Content* includes the topics, subjects, or issues; *process* is about how the topics, subjects, or issues are addressed.

Celebrating Successes

Because communications from managers and supervisors have been shown to have a significant impact on employees during a change initiative, it is appropriate that they be actively involved in celebrating success with employees as a result of positive performance. Celebrations can occur on three levels:

Level 1 - One on one conversation: In a private meeting, a supervisor should attest to the fact that due to the employee's effort, a change was made, and how it is succeeding. He or she should extend verbal thanks to the employee.

Level 2 - Public recognition: Public recognition officially acknowledges outstanding performance and points out a role model that helped make a successful change happen. Supervisors should carefully consider who receives recognition, and not alienate group members who participated in the change but who many not have distinguished themselves as significantly.

Level 3 - Group celebrations: Fun or engaging activities are used to celebrate key milestones by a group. They include buffet or restaurant lunches, dinner events, or can include group outings to sports, amusement, or cultural events. It is important that these types of celebrations try to include the involvement of the primary change sponsor in some way.

The exercise below that draws upon experiences from the change management class is an example of a group celebration that might precede a lunch, dinner, our outing.

Sharing the Results and Benefits

In order to sustain the impact of a change, it is important for everyone who is involved in the process to know what results are occurring. This occurs across a number of dimensions.

Ongoing feedback is needed from employees at all levels. Feedback tools such as the Feedback at Contemporary Chemical form in the Evaluating and Adapting section of Module 6 remain a good method for gathering ongoing input. Using an electronic delivery method improves throughput.

Chapter 7 – Using Appreciative Inquiry

Appreciative inquiry is a model for change management developed by David L. Cooperrider, Ph.D., a professor at Case Western University. The name combines two definitions:

- **Appreciate**: to look for the best in something, and to increase something in value.

- **Inquiry** means to seek understanding using a process based on provocative questions.

Based on the meanings of the two words, AI theorizes that organizations are not problems to be solved. Rather, each organization has been created as a solution, designed in its own time, to meet a challenge, or to satisfy a need within society.

A guiding principle in appreciative inquiry is the concept of the positive core, or what gives life to an organization. Below is a list of elements that make up a positive core.

Achievements, strategic opportunities, cooperative moments, technical assets, innovations, elevated thoughts, community assets, positive emotions, financial assets, community wisdom, core competencies, visions of possibility, vital traditions and values, positive macro trends, social capital, and embedded knowledge.

The Four Stages

The four stages in the Appreciative Inquiry model are known as the 4-D cycle. They are:

Stage 1 Discovery: Mobilizing the whole system by engaging all stakeholders in the articulation of strengths and best practices. Identifying "The best of what has been and what is."

Stage 2 Dream: Creating a clear results-oriented vision in relation to discovered potential and in relation to questions of higher purpose, such as "What does the world call us to become?"

Stage 3 Design: Creating possibility propositions of the idea organization, articulating an organization design that is capable of drawing upon and magnifying the positive core to realize the newly expressed dream.

Stage 4 Destiny: Strengthening the affirmative capability of the whole system, enabling it to build hope and sustain momentum for ongoing positive change and high performance.

While each AI process is unique in an organization, change efforts typically progress sequentially through the 4-D cycle. Positioned in the center of the diagram below, the organization's **Affirmative Topic Choice** is entered, surrounded by the four phases.

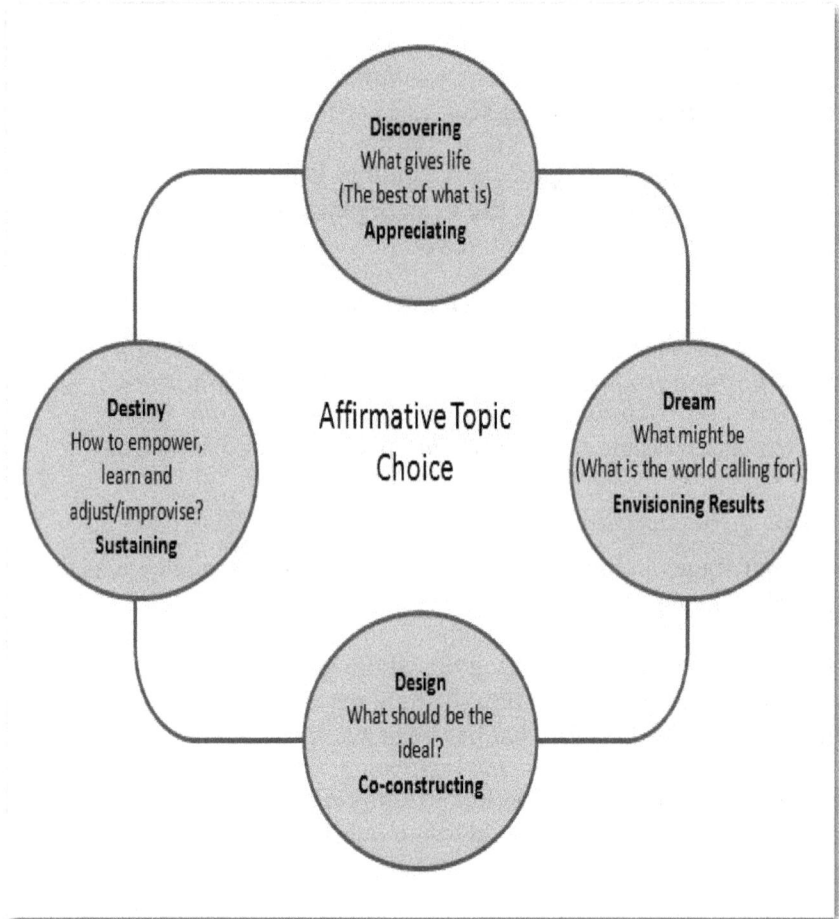

Various types of questions help elicit feedback and ideas during the process:

- What's the biggest problem here?

- Why do we still have those problems?

- What possibilities exist that we have not yet considered?

- What's the smallest change that could make the biggest impact?

- What solutions would have us both win?

Topics emerge from interviews with people throughout the organization in several ways.

- Preliminary interviews are held within the organization at its best levels

- A cross-section of people throughout the organization are engaged in inquiry

- People are challenged to shift deficit (negative) issues into affirmative (positive) topics for inquiry.

The Purposes of Appreciative Inquiry

Appreciative inquiry is conducted in organizations for several reasons.

- It allows the performance of people from across the whole system to participate in an inquiry; all stakeholders (employees, customers, vendors, and interested community members) are involved in the process.

- It leads to the design of appreciative organizations that can support stakeholders fostering a triple bottom line; people, profits, and planet.

- It serves as a catalyst for the transformation of an organizational culture.

Examples and Case Studies

Over the past twenty years, there have been many approaches to appreciative inquiry. Two key methods of the appreciative inquiry used often in organizations are **Whole System Inquiry** and the **AI Summit**.

Whole-System Inquiry

Whole-System Inquiry follows the 4-D cycle to involve all stakeholders (employees, customers, vendors, and interested community members) in the appreciative inquiry process.

Cycle Phase(s)	Methods
Discovery	Interviews by facilitators Interviews of each other
Dream, Design, and Destiny	During these three phases, small groups gather to: • share stories • capture best practices • launch teams to address innovation or other issues that have arisen

The AI Summit

The AI Summit is a full-scale meeting process that concentrates on the discovery and development of an organization's positive core. The process participants then use this knowledge to design strategic business processes (marketing, customer service, leadership, human resources development, new products). Cross sections of diverse stakeholders participate.

Typically a four-day event, each day focuses on one of the cycle phases.

Day	Cycle Phase(s)	Focus	Participants
1	Discovery	Perform a system-wide inquiry into the core	• Hold appreciative interviews • Capture, reflect on interview highlights
2	Dream	Imagine the organization's greatest potential for positive influence and effect in the world	• Share dreams captured during the interviews • Create and present dramatic enactments
3	Design	Create propositions that reflect a boldly alive positive core in all strategies, processes, systems, decisions, and collaborations	• Create provocative design statements, incorporating the positive core
4	Destiny	Invite action inspired by the discovery, dream and design days	• Declare intended actions publicly and ask for support • Use self-organized groups to plan next steps

Roadway Express

In 2000, Roadway Express, a leading transporter of industrial, commercial, and retail goods decided to drive down costs and increase business by creating an organization that expressed leadership at every level. At facilities around their network, drivers, dock workers, and office workers and professionals at all levels would join senior management at annual strategic planning sessions, learn the business, and create new levels of partnership between the unions and the company. Appreciative inquiry was chosen as the change methodology.

At many AI Summits, Roadway looked to increase employee leadership empowerment to increase net profit margins of 5%. At a

Summit held at a Winston-Salem, NC terminal, a team of short-haul drivers generated twelve cost-cutting measures. For example, if each of 32 drivers made only one extra delivery per hour, that would result in 288 additional daily shipments.

In first quarter 2003, Roadway reported that their fourth quarter revenues were up 25.7 percent versus the same quarter one year earlier. During the AI Summit process, Roadway stock increased from $14 per share to $40 per share.

When Roadway merged with Yellow to form the new YRC Company, the AI Summit was selected as the vehicle to propel the merger integration to a higher level. As of 2005, more than ten thousand people at YRC had participated in at least one AI Summit. A new electronic and virtual architecture called the Core Strength Network has allowed employees to spread innovation and best practices throughout the organization. Now using virtual meetings with the Network, the company has redesigned the dock in Akron, allowed drivers the opportunity to become successful salespersons, and encouraged one terminal to become the highest margin facility in the company. New software called OvationNet is now taking the online knowledge sharing and collaboration to the next level.

British Airways

In 1999, David Erich, V.P. of Customer Service for British Airways North America wanted to engage employees to make changes to increase work satisfaction and to provide the level of customer service for which the airline is known worldwide. In North America, it was found that best practices were not being identified, shared, or replicated across the 22 stations. Mr. Erich undertook a whole-system appreciative inquiry process to transform the organizational culture.

After several preliminary briefings and meetings where more than fifty line managers and organizational development professionals learned about appreciative inquiry and checked with colleagues in two other companies, a full-scale appreciative inquiry initiative was launched.

During a pivotal core team meeting where affirmative inquiry topics were being selected, the issue of the cost and frustrations of delayed and lost baggage emerged. However upon further exploration by the facilitators, it was determined that the ability of customer service agents to provide an exceptional arrival experience would be a more positive focus. Three other topics agreed to were happiness at work, continuous people development, and harmony among work groups.

Two initiatives would be required in order to effect positive change with the four topics: management commitment and the involvement of the entire workforce. This meant that a whole-system involvement would be needed to achieve the goals.

With the agreement of the core team to steward the process, volunteers signed up for roles including:

- Conducting interviews

- Naming and branding the initiative

- Speaking about AI to groups

- Writing articles or being interviewed for in-house communications

- Serving as the AI coordinator at the station.

A cross-level, cross-functional steering team that included an AI consultant was formed to oversee the issues and team progress. The process was given a name, "The Power of Two", and the AI initiative took off at British Airways.

Typical of the questions that were asked were:

- Describe your most memorable arrival experience, as a customer or, as airline personnel. What made it memorable for you? How did you feel?

- Tell me a story about your most powerful service recovery. Describe the situation. What was it about you that made it happen?

- Who else was involved and why was he or she significant?

- What tools did you use or what did you do that others might be able to do when in a similar situation?

The Imagine Chicago project

A third case involves a non-profit community organization in Chicago. Imagine Chicago was founded by Bliss Browne in 1992 to help people imagine and create a positive future for Chicago and its children. Its first project was a city-wide appreciative inquiry process in which 50 at risk youths interviewed more than 150 adult community builders in Chicago to learn about the highlights of their lives as citizens -- and their hopes and plans for the city's future.

During a five-month period, several different strategies were used:

- Provide training to citizen leaders about the appreciative inquiry process

- Learning to ask positive questions

- Team formation and organization strategies

- Brainstorming strategies to determine project focuses

- Action planning

- Implementation and sustaining strategies.

IMAGINE Chicago's AI work involved three core processes:

1. Dialogue -- across cultural, racial, and generational boundaries

2. Curriculum development -- frameworks and organizers to understand, imagine and create projects that build community

3. Network formation -- to link individuals and organizations committed to developing a positive future for Chicago and its children.

As a result of the AI project consisting mainly of intergenerational interviews, Imagine Chicago leaders discovered that commitments of the adult community citizens were rejuvenated, a new sense of shared civic identify was cultivated, and young people felt a greater commitment toward making a difference.

Chapter 8 – Bringing People to Your Side

Leadership in change management involves aligning people with an organization's issue or need, allowing them to see that they are working together toward an important cause.

A Dash of Emotion

Emotion is defined as a state of feeling. Because change in organizations doesn't happen without people, human elements and emotion cannot be downplayed. As an organization works with the appreciative inquiry process, six essential conditions come together in an organization. They liberate personal and organizational power, resulting in a transformation for the people in the organization.

1. **Freedom to be known in relationship**: The nature of the appreciative inquiry process leads people to feel encouraged to shine as individuals, not just as someone performing a role.

2. **Freedom to be heard:** Through the interview process, individuals gain the freedom to be heard.

3. **Freedom to dream in community**: People feel more free and in a safe place to share dreams as they dialogue together.

4. **Freedom to choose to contribute:** People feel empowered in an appreciative inquiry environment, and assume commitments they might not otherwise undertake.

5. **Freedom to act with support:** The awareness that others care about their work makes individuals comfortable experimenting with new ideas.

6. **Freedom to be positive:** Suddenly, the environment validates the fact that it is acceptable to have fun. People feel positive and proud of their work experiences.

Plenty of Facts

A fact is something that is demonstrated to exist, or known to have existed. As opposed to the "people" component, emotion, facts are straightforward, and necessary to measure progress. As a change management project shifts into the launch or in-process stage, the change management team must make sure that measurement is ongoing. Two types of measurements are described below.

- **Audits and performance measurement systems:** Audits and measurement systems provide data to determine the adoption rate of change. They help to determine:

- How many employees are using the new processes or systems?

- Individual or group proficiency levels

- Who is not engaged with the process, or is struggling, and why?

Formal, quantitative assessment instruments and a review of performance data provide this information. The results allow the change management and/or project teams to develop and implement corrective actions, make modifications to the program, or use positive results to propel to the project forward.

- **Accountability Systems:** Enhancements should be made to performance evaluation and compensation systems in order to maintain the accountability and credibility of the change. This is important in order to maintain ongoing reinforcement of the changed systems or processes.

Chapter 9 – Building Resiliency

Resiliency is the capacity to absorb high levels of change while maintaining a level of performance and displaying minimal dysfunctional behavior.

People who are resilient do two things to reduce their susceptibility to dysfunctional behavior during change: They increase their capacity to absorb shock, and they reduce the amount of effort necessary to successfully implement any one change.

What is Resiliency?

Resilience isn't an absolute characteristic; rather it is a combination of traits of varying degrees in people. Resilient people, whom psychologist Daryl Conner terms O-Type, perceive more opportunity than non-resilient people do. They approach life as meaningful, and as a guiding beacon through the challenges of change. Their optimistic view lets them see each new day as providing a new set of opportunities and choices; they view disruption as a necessary part of adjusting to the challenges of change.

In contrast to O-Type individuals, D-Types perceive danger; they are individuals who use defense mechanisms such as denial, distortion, and delusions to deflect change and are reactive. The opposite O-Type individuals are proactive, and understand when to ask for help.

Why is It Important?

When resilient people are confronted with ambiguity, anxiety, and a loss of control that accompanies change, they tend to grow stronger from the experiences, rather than allowing themselves to be depleted. Resilient people are more likely to make a quicker and more effective adaptation to change. They are winners, rather than losers, critically important in organizations. Resilient people are necessary to foster success during a change.

While no person is specifically O-Type or D-Type, people with O-Type characteristics tend to exhibit a high degree of resilience. This allows them to understand that the future contains constantly shifting variables, display willingness to explore paradoxes, and stay the course during periods of significant disruption.

People shift between sides on a resilience continuum, depending upon the characteristics being exhibited, and the change being experienced.

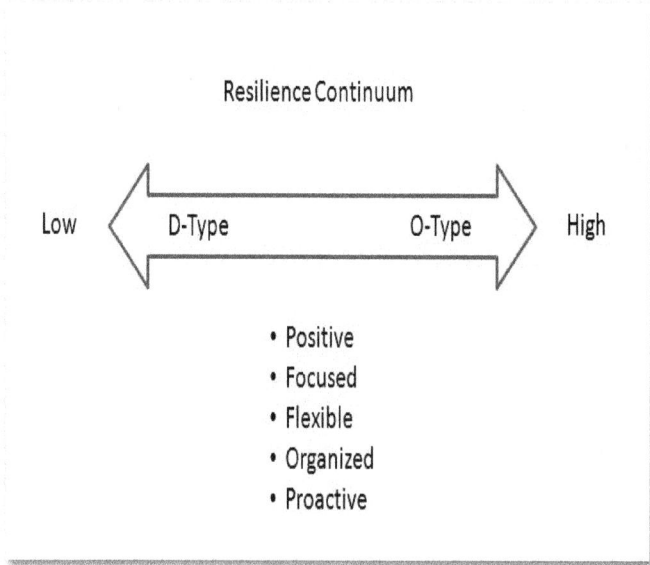

Resilience Continuum

Low   D-Type   O-Type   High

- Positive
- Focused
- Flexible
- Organized
- Proactive

Five Easy Steps for the Leader and the Individual

One can practice behaviors and steps to become more resilient. Below are some steps leaders and individuals can take to foster resilience?

Step 1: Develop a more Positive world view and self-concept

- Notice what you say to yourself in an unfamiliar situation

- Find specific opportunities during challenges you face

- Practice turning minuses into pluses

- Take a time out during a period of frustration

- Look for a positive person to serve as your coach

Step 2: Maintain a Focused sense of purpose for long-term goals and priorities

- Explore your value system and identify your personal sense of direction on which you can rely to make choices

- Set new priorities when faced with the disruption of change

Step 3: Use Flexible thinking to explore multiple approaches for addressing uncertainty.

- Switch sides when discussing a topic about which you feel strongly

- Rather than assuming your first answer is the solution, suspend judgment if you are in the middle of a change

- List three positives and three negatives about a new idea or concept

- Be willing to work in an unfamiliar role to learn a different point of view

- Identify a person who is a strong flexible thinker, and ask for some coaching

Step 4: Use Organized, structured approaches when managing ambiguity

- Learn to quickly sort information and find patterns in new situations

- Use a planner or planning software to keep to-do lists, track plans, commitments, and next steps for each change initiative

- Break down complex or ambiguous situations into manageable chunks

- Find a coach who has strong organizational skills.

Step 5: Experiment proactively with new approaches and solutions

- Choose a small project and experiment with a new approach

- For a challenge you face, define the worst-case scenario; list how you would address each risk

- Find someone you perceive as a successful risk-taker and discuss your objections and concerns about a change

- Try to view a risk associated with a change you are facing as a "win-win" situation; determine what you can learn by assuming the risk

- Find a coach who excels at proactive experimentation.

Chapter 10 – Building Flexibility

Being flexible on personal and social levels is critical for individuals involved in or leading a change to be able to make shifts as necessary during a project.

What is Flexibility?

There are two dimensions of flexibility; flexible thinking, and social flexibility.

Flexible Thinking: People who think flexibly can generate a broad range of thoughts and possible responses without feeling compelled to decide on one response right away. They have a tolerance for ambiguity plus a high level of creativity. This allows them to tackle a problem from many directions.

Flexible thinkers enjoy new or complex ideas, are open to varying perspectives, and devise creative solutions in order to adapt to change. At a personal level, people who think flexibly supplement their own knowledge with the talents of other people, knowing they themselves cannot have all the answers. They are facile at building networks to freely exchange support and information.

Social Flexibility: People with a great degree of social flexibility have a clear sense of their individual strengths and weaknesses. Their self-concept is not easily threatened as they reach out to others, looking for collaboration and working to build social networks. They have no problem reaching out to see where others can add value and asking others for support.

Why is it Important?

Flexible people are team players, a critical need during a change management initiative. Flexibility allows one to brainstorm more efficiently, bringing a wider range of ideas to a project team. The broad range of solutions brought to the table by a flexible thinker encourages a strong change solution -- and avoids the potential for inferior solutions that may be generated by people with low levels of social flexibility.

Five Easy Steps for the Leader and the Individual

The following five steps can benefit either a leader or an individual who is dealing with change on a personal or an organizational level.

Personal Level	Social Level
Swap sides in a discussion on a topic about which you feel strongly.	Identify colleagues who have a different view than you, and ask their opinions.
Suspend judgment during a change. Don't assume that the first answer is the best or only one.	If a colleague presents an idea that seems off-base to you, take a step back and try to see the rationale from your colleague's point of view.
Practice thinking of paradoxes (both/and) rather than contradictions (either/or). Try to generate both positives and negatives about a new idea or concept, rather than focusing exclusively on one or another. Listen to others.	Ask colleagues or friends for their opinions about your thoughts regarding a change; listen completely to their answers and avoid passing judgment on their contributions.
Offer to work in a role that's unfamiliar to you so you can approach a situation from a different point of view.	Pinpoint a skill you want to learn; ask someone to help you learn it.
Find someone who is strong in flexible thinking to serve as your coach.	Identify someone who is adept with social flexibility and ask for coaching.

Additional Titles

The 90 Minute Guide series of books covers a variety of general business skills and are intended to be completed in 90 minutes or less. It is an effective way for building your skill set and can be used to acquire professional development units needed by project managers and other industries to maintain their certification. For the availability of titles please see

https://www.silvercitypublications.com/shop/.

No. 1 - Appreciative Inquiry

No. 2 - Assertiveness and Self Control

No. 3 - Attention Management

No. 4 - Body Language Basics

No. 5 - Business Acumen

No. 6 - Business and Etiquette

No. 7 - Change Management

No. 8 - Coaching and Mentoring

No. 9 - Communications Strategies

No. 10 - Conflict Resolution

www.ingramcontent.com/pod-product-compliance
Lightning Source LLC
Chambersburg PA
CBHW060502210326
41520CB00015B/4058